IMPORTANT INFO

THIS JOURNAL:

- Gives information that is educational and as general information.
- This is for the reader's own self care and to improve themselves.
- Is not intended to diagnose, treat, cure or take place of any recommendations your doctor or counselor given you.
- Is not to replace medical care or mental health care.
- Gives information about EFT (Emotional Freedom Technique).

EFT:

- Is based on Eastern medicine (acupuncture), using our body's meridian and energy.
- Gives us the ability to balance our energy and help it to flow better.
- Is done by gently tapping on meridian points on the body.
- It is a simple, easy, and relaxing process.
- Gives us the opportunity to work through emotions and feelings that create stress and anxiety in our bodies.
- Tapping helps us get back into balance . . . naturally.
- Very helpful and effective to help to reduce anxiety, stress and other issues.
- Process is still considered as experimental & cannot make healing claims.

USING THIS BOOK:

- You assume responsibility for all risks by using this method and this book.
- If you experience any discomfort while tapping, physical or emotional, you are advised to stop and get medical treatment.
- You understand the author of this book is a certified EFT Practitioner, not a licensed health care provider.
- The author doesn't guarantee an outcome and isn't responsible for any unwanted effects from the content in this book.
- By continuing reading this book, you agree to release the author from any claim, liability or damage that occurs while using this book.

Being consistent and listening to your body will help you to make progress in your journey.

This Journal Belongs to:

_____

Getting Started

WHAT IS EFT?

EFT, the **Emotional Freedom Technique**, is also known as 'tapping'. It's like psychological acupressure, a very unique method, that has the potential to help with many **emotional and physical issues**.

It is believed that emotions, stress, and trauma is **stuck energy** in our body. Tapping on specific points on our body can help to get this negative energy "unstuck".

I know it may sound "woo-woo", but I have experienced it first-hand the changes both physically and emotionally.

Some experts explain trauma as a memory or emotion that gets stuck or trapped in our nervous system and in our minds. Trauma and memories can leave an impression on our brain, like a stamp making an imprint on our mind.

This makes sense because we all have memories in our past that pop-up for us when we find ourselves in certain situations, **reliving past situations or memories.**

Learning this simple, safe and effective tool can help anyone to deal with a variety of issues, both physically and emotionally.

I **don't** recommend that anyone ever **substitute** tapping (EFT) for medical advice or counseling. This can be an additional tool.

BENEFITS OF EFT

EFT offers great benefits including:

- Non-evasive
- **Simple and easy**
- Can't do it "wrong"
- **Can learn it in a short period of time**
- Can do it any time and anywhere
- **A powerful tool that can have lasting effects**
- The side effects are almost always positive

EFT doesn't heal or "cure" things. However, it can help make big changes like **relieving stress** that is related to past memories, worrying, anxiety or negative thoughts.

I have read about some who have had physical benefits, like releasing pain.

DON'T substitute your **physician's guidance** with tapping. You can discuss with them how it can be used along with your current care.

DON'T substitute your **counselor's guidance** with tapping. For serious issues such as trauma, like PTSD, talk to your counselor about how this technique can be used along side with your care plan. (Vets and victims of horrible crimes have benefitted greatly from this process)

HOW TO DO EFT

THE BASICS OF THE PROCESS

- State the fear/memory/emotion you want to work on.
- **Try to identify the true reason behind the emotion or fear.**
- Go back to the most recent memory when you had the issue or stress around it.
- **Create a target statement to solve the memory/fear using your own words and any physical reactions.**
- How do you react/feel physically and emotionally when you think of this issue?
- **Measure the intensity of the issue/memory/fear on a scale of 0-10.**
- Tap on the points to eliminate the issue/memory/fear. Repeat as often as necessary.

TAPPING TIPS

- When tapping you can use one or two hands.
- **Points don't have to be perfectly tapped on.**
- Can't do it "wrong".
- **Tapping on points are done while repeating statements.**
- Assess how you feel about the issue you are tapping about, before and after.
- **There are no rules about how long to tap. Tap until your issue is gone. In one sitting or many.**

TAPPING POINTS

These photos will help you to better understand the points and how you use the ends of your fingers. You do not need to tap hard to get results.

Karate Chop - KC

Eyebrow - EB

Side of Eye - SE

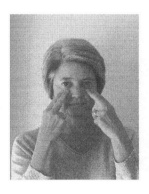

Under the Eye - UE

Under the Nose - UN

Chin - C

Collarbone - CB

Under the Arm - UA

Top of Head - TH

SCRIPT #1

Release Stress Tapping Script

Karate Chop (KC): (Set-up Statement)
- Even though I feel overwhelmed and stressed, I deeply love and accept myself.
- Even though I am not sure how I am going to handle this stress, I deeply love and accept myself.
- Even though I am tired of feeling stressed and overwhelmed, I deeply love accept myself and forgive myself.

Eyebrow (EB): It is overwhelming the stress that I feel.
Side of Eye (SE): This stress can be so overwhelming.
Under Eye (UE): How am I going to keep it together?
Under Nose (UN): I don't think I can handle all this stress.
Chin (C): I don't have the time or energy to be stressed out.
Collar Bone (CB): I don't understand why this happens.
Under Arm (UA): I am holding onto something I have no control over.
Top of Head (TH): It feels like others don't struggle like I do.

Eyebrow (EB): I want to let go of this stress and anxiety.
Side of Eye (SE): It's not helping the situation and I feel angry I can't fix this.
Under Eye (UE): Releasing the stress will help me to feel better.
Under Nose (UN): If I am relaxed, I can feel better and not feel paralyzed.
Chin (C): I'm tired of the stress and want to release it, it's not serving me.
Collar Bone (CB): I am releasing the stress.
Under Arm (UA): I am releasing the worry and stress.
Top of Head (TH): And I am allowing myself to understand that this will get resolved, and I can let go of all the stress.

Deep Breath.

SCRIPT #2

Anxiety Tapping Script

Karate Chop (KC): (Set-up Statement)
- Even though this anxiety is overwhelming, I deeply love and accept myself.
- Even though I don't know how I can get rid of this anxiety that feels paralyzing, I deeply love and accept myself.
- Even though I just want to tune out and try to try and feel better about the situation, I deeply love accept myself and forgive myself.

Eyebrow (EB): Anxiety is a horrible feeling, and I'm feeling out of control.
Side of Eye (SE): I don't feel like I can be myself, I have to hide this horrible feeling.
Under Eye (UE): I don't know how to make this better.
Under Nose (UN): Anxiety keeps me from being myself.
Chin (C): It all feels so out of control and I don't know how to fix this.
Collar Bone (CB): Why won't this go away, it makes me so upset.
Under Arm (UA): I'm tired of feeling this way, it's hard to stay focused.
Top of Head (TH): I really need to get rid of this anxiety.

Eyebrow (EB): I wish I knew why I felt this way.
Side of Eye (SE): I need clarity about why I feel out of control.
Under Eye (UE): I am giving myself permission to relax.
Under Nose (UN): If I am relaxed, I can feel better and not feel paralyzed.
Chin (C): I'm letting go of my anxiety, it's not helping to hold it in.
Collar Bone (CB): I don't have to control things.
Under Arm (UA): It can work out without me being involved.
Top of Head (TH): And I am willing accept that I don't need to control situations even when they don't go as planned.

Deep Breath.

My difficult memories, trauma and disappointments: _____

_____

_____

_____

_____

_____

_____

_____

_____

_____

_____

_____

_____

_____

_____

_____

_____

_____

_____

Journal Entries

Date: _____

What issues, feelings, anxiety or stress am I experiencing right now?

_____

_____

_____

_____

_____

_____

_____

_____

Tapping Topic: _____

_____

Rating Before Tapping (0-10): _____

Rating After Tapping (0-10): _____

What feelings or emotions came up for me while tapping?

_____

_____

_____

_____

_____

_____

_____

_____

Second Round Tapping Topic: _____

_____

Rating Before Tapping (0-10): _____

Rating After Tapping (0-10): _____

What feelings or emotions came up for me? _____

_____

_____

_____

_____

_____

_____

_____

_____

_____

What other issues that came up for me while tapping?_____

_____

_____

_____

_____

_____

_____

_____

What do I want to tap about next time? _____

_____

_____

_____

_____

_____

Notes: _____

_____

_____

_____

_____

_____

_____

_____

_____

_____

_____

_____

_____

_____

_____

Date: _____

What issues, feelings, anxiety or stress am I experiencing right now?

_____

_____

_____

_____

_____

_____

_____

_____

Tapping Topic: _____

_____

Rating Before Tapping (0-10): _____

Rating After Tapping (0-10): _____

What feelings or emotions came up for me while tapping?

_____

_____

_____

_____

_____

_____

_____

Second Round Tapping Topic: _____

_____

Rating Before Tapping (0-10): _____

Rating After Tapping (0-10): _____

What feelings or emotions came up for me? _____

_____

_____

_____

_____

_____

_____

_____

_____

_____

What other issues that came up for me while tapping?_____

_____

_____

_____

_____

_____

_____

What do I want to tap about next time? _____

_____

_____

_____

_____

_____

_____

Notes: _____

_____

_____

_____

_____

_____

_____

_____

_____

_____

_____

_____

_____

_____

Date: _____

What issues, feelings, anxiety or stress am I experiencing right now?

_____

_____

_____

_____

_____

_____

_____

_____

Tapping Topic: _____

_____

Rating Before Tapping (0-10): _____

Rating After Tapping (0-10): _____

What feelings or emotions came up for me while tapping?

_____

_____

_____

_____

_____

_____

_____

_____

Second Round Tapping Topic: _____

_____

Rating Before Tapping (0-10): _____

Rating After Tapping (0-10): _____

What feelings or emotions came up for me? _____

_____

_____

_____

_____

_____

_____

_____

_____

_____

_____

What other issues that came up for me while tapping?_____

_____

_____

_____

_____

_____

_____

_____

What do I want to tap about next time? _____

_____

_____

_____

_____

_____

Notes:_____

_____

_____

_____

_____

_____

_____

_____

_____

_____

_____

_____

_____

Date: _____

What issues, feelings, anxiety or stress am I experiencing right now?

_____

_____

_____

_____

_____

_____

_____

Tapping Topic: _____

_____

Rating Before Tapping (0-10): _____

Rating After Tapping (0-10): _____

What feelings or emotions came up for me while tapping?

_____

_____

_____

_____

_____

_____

_____

Second Round Tapping Topic: _____

_____

Rating Before Tapping (0-10): _____

Rating After Tapping (0-10): _____

What feelings or emotions came up for me? _____

_____

_____

_____

_____

_____

_____

_____

_____

_____

What other issues that came up for me while tapping?_____

_____

_____

_____

_____

_____

_____

_____

What do I want to tap about next time? _____

_____

_____

_____

_____

_____

Notes:_____

_____

_____

_____

_____

_____

_____

_____

_____

_____

_____

_____

_____

Date: _____

What issues, feelings, anxiety or stress am I experiencing right now?

_____

_____

_____

_____

_____

_____

_____

_____

Tapping Topic: _____

_____

Rating Before Tapping (0-10): _____

Rating After Tapping (0-10): _____

What feelings or emotions came up for me while tapping?

_____

_____

_____

_____

_____

_____

Second Round Tapping Topic: _____

_____

Rating Before Tapping (0-10): _____

Rating After Tapping (0-10): _____

What feelings or emotions came up for me? _____

_____

_____

_____

_____

_____

_____

_____

_____

_____

What other issues that came up for me while tapping?_____

_____

_____

_____

_____

_____

_____

_____

What do I want to tap about next time? _____

_____

_____

_____

_____

_____

Notes: _____

_____

_____

_____

_____

_____

_____

_____

_____

_____

_____

_____

_____

_____

Date: _____

What issues, feelings, anxiety or stress am I experiencing right now?

_____

_____

_____

_____

_____

_____

_____

_____

Tapping Topic: _____

_____

Rating Before Tapping (0-10): _____

Rating After Tapping (0-10): _____

What feelings or emotions came up for me while tapping?

_____

_____

_____

_____

_____

_____

_____

_____

Second Round Tapping Topic: _____

_____

Rating Before Tapping (0-10): _____

Rating After Tapping (0-10): _____

What feelings or emotions came up for me? _____

_____

_____

_____

_____

_____

_____

_____

_____

_____

What other issues that came up for me while tapping?_____

_____

_____

_____

_____

_____

_____

What do I want to tap about next time? _____

_____

_____

_____

_____

_____

Notes: _____

_____

_____

_____

_____

_____

_____

_____

_____

_____

_____

_____

_____

_____

_____

Date: _____

What issues, feelings, anxiety or stress am I experiencing right now?

_____

_____

_____

_____

_____

_____

_____

_____

Tapping Topic: _____

_____

Rating Before Tapping (0-10): _____

Rating After Tapping (0-10): _____

What feelings or emotions came up for me while tapping?

_____

_____

_____

_____

_____

_____

_____

Second Round Tapping Topic: _____

_____

Rating Before Tapping (0-10): _____

Rating After Tapping (0-10): _____

What feelings or emotions came up for me? _____

_____

_____

_____

_____

_____

_____

_____

_____

_____

What other issues that came up for me while tapping? _____

_____

_____

_____

_____

_____

_____

What do I want to tap about next time? _____

_____

_____

_____

_____

_____

Notes: _____

_____

_____

_____

_____

_____

_____

_____

_____

_____

_____

_____

_____

_____

Date: _____

What issues, feelings, anxiety or stress am I experiencing right now?

_____

_____

_____

_____

_____

_____

_____

Tapping Topic: _____

_____

Rating Before Tapping (0-10): _____

Rating After Tapping (0-10): _____

What feelings or emotions came up for me while tapping?

_____

_____

_____

_____

_____

_____

_____

Second Round Tapping Topic: _____

_____

Rating Before Tapping (0-10): _____

Rating After Tapping (0-10): _____

What feelings or emotions came up for me? _____

_____

_____

_____

_____

_____

_____

_____

_____

_____

What other issues that came up for me while tapping?_____

_____

_____

_____

_____

_____

_____

_____

What do I want to tap about next time? _____

_____

_____

_____

_____

_____

Notes: _____

_____

_____

_____

_____

_____

_____

_____

_____

_____

_____

_____

_____

_____

Date: _____

What issues, feelings, anxiety or stress am I experiencing right now?

_____

_____

_____

_____

_____

_____

_____

_____

Tapping Topic: _____

_____

Rating Before Tapping (0-10): _____

Rating After Tapping (0-10): _____

What feelings or emotions came up for me while tapping?

_____

_____

_____

_____

_____

_____

_____

Second Round Tapping Topic: _____

_____

Rating Before Tapping (0-10): _____

Rating After Tapping (0-10): _____

What feelings or emotions came up for me? _____

_____

_____

_____

_____

_____

_____

_____

_____

_____

What other issues that came up for me while tapping?_____

_____

_____

_____

_____

_____

_____

_____

What do I want to tap about next time? _____

_____

_____

_____

_____

_____

Notes: _____

_____

_____

_____

_____

_____

_____

_____

_____

_____

_____

_____

_____

_____

Date: _____

What issues, feelings, anxiety or stress am I experiencing right now?

_____

_____

_____

_____

_____

_____

_____

_____

Tapping Topic: _____

_____

Rating Before Tapping (0-10): _____

Rating After Tapping (0-10): _____

What feelings or emotions came up for me while tapping?

_____

_____

_____

_____

_____

_____

_____

Second Round Tapping Topic: _____

_____

Rating Before Tapping (0-10): _____

Rating After Tapping (0-10): _____

What feelings or emotions came up for me? _____

_____

_____

_____

_____

_____

_____

_____

_____

_____

What other issues that came up for me while tapping?_____

_____

_____

_____

_____

_____

_____

What do I want to tap about next time? _____

_____

_____

_____

_____

_____

_____

Notes: _____

_____

_____

_____

_____

_____

_____

_____

_____

_____

_____

_____

_____

_____

Date: _____

What issues, feelings, anxiety or stress am I experiencing right now?

_____

_____

_____

_____

_____

_____

_____

Tapping Topic: _____

_____

Rating Before Tapping (0-10): _____

Rating After Tapping (0-10): _____

What feelings or emotions came up for me while tapping?

_____

_____

_____

_____

_____

_____

_____

Second Round Tapping Topic: _____

_____

Rating Before Tapping (0-10): _____

Rating After Tapping (0-10): _____

What feelings or emotions came up for me? _____

_____

_____

_____

_____

_____

_____

_____

_____

What other issues that came up for me while tapping?_____

_____

_____

_____

_____

_____

_____

_____

What do I want to tap about next time? _____

_____

_____

_____

_____

_____

Notes:_____

_____

_____

_____

_____

_____

_____

_____

_____

_____

_____

_____

_____

_____

Date: _____

What issues, feelings, anxiety or stress am I experiencing right now?

_____

_____

_____

_____

_____

_____

_____

_____

Tapping Topic: _____

_____

Rating Before Tapping (0-10): _____

Rating After Tapping (0-10): _____

What feelings or emotions came up for me while tapping?

_____

_____

_____

_____

_____

_____

_____

Second Round Tapping Topic: _____

_____

Rating Before Tapping (0-10): _____

Rating After Tapping (0-10): _____

What feelings or emotions came up for me? _____

_____

_____

_____

_____

_____

_____

_____

_____

_____

What other issues that came up for me while tapping? _____

_____

_____

_____

_____

_____

_____

_____

What do I want to tap about next time? _____

_____

_____

_____

_____

_____

Notes: _____

_____

_____

_____

_____

_____

_____

_____

_____

_____

_____

_____

_____

_____

Date: _____

What issues, feelings, anxiety or stress am I experiencing right now?

_____

_____

_____

_____

_____

_____

_____

_____

Tapping Topic: _____

_____

Rating Before Tapping (0-10): _____

Rating After Tapping (0-10): _____

What feelings or emotions came up for me while tapping?

_____

_____

_____

_____

_____

_____

_____

_____

Second Round Tapping Topic: _____

_____

Rating Before Tapping (0-10): _____

Rating After Tapping (0-10): _____

What feelings or emotions came up for me? _____

_____

_____

_____

_____

_____

_____

_____

_____

_____

What other issues that came up for me while tapping?_____

_____

_____

_____

_____

_____

_____

_____

What do I want to tap about next time? _____

_____

_____

_____

_____

_____

Notes: _____

Date: _____

What issues, feelings, anxiety or stress am I experiencing right now?

_____

_____

_____

_____

_____

_____

_____

Tapping Topic: _____

_____

Rating Before Tapping (0-10): _____

Rating After Tapping (0-10): _____

What feelings or emotions came up for me while tapping?

_____

_____

_____

_____

_____

_____

_____

Second Round Tapping Topic: _____

_____

Rating Before Tapping (0-10): _____

Rating After Tapping (0-10): _____

What feelings or emotions came up for me? _____

_____

_____

_____

_____

_____

_____

_____

_____

_____

What other issues that came up for me while tapping?_____

_____

_____

_____

_____

_____

_____

_____

What do I want to tap about next time? _____

_____

_____

_____

_____

_____

Notes: _____

_____

_____

_____

_____

_____

_____

_____

_____

_____

_____

_____

_____

_____

_____

Date: _____

What issues, feelings, anxiety or stress am I experiencing right now?

_____

_____

_____

_____

_____

_____

_____

_____

Tapping Topic: _____

_____

Rating Before Tapping (0-10): _____

Rating After Tapping (0-10): _____

What feelings or emotions came up for me while tapping?

_____

_____

_____

_____

_____

_____

_____

Second Round Tapping Topic: _____

_____

Rating Before Tapping (0-10): _____

Rating After Tapping (0-10): _____

What feelings or emotions came up for me? _____

_____

_____

_____

_____

_____

_____

_____

_____

_____

What other issues that came up for me while tapping?_____

_____

_____

_____

_____

_____

_____

_____

What do I want to tap about next time? _____

_____

_____

_____

_____

_____

Notes: _____

_____

_____

_____

_____

_____

_____

_____

_____

_____

_____

_____

_____

_____

Date: _____

What issues, feelings, anxiety or stress am I experiencing right now?

_____

_____

_____

_____

_____

_____

_____

_____

Tapping Topic: _____

_____

Rating Before Tapping (0-10): _____

Rating After Tapping (0-10): _____

What feelings or emotions came up for me while tapping?

_____

_____

_____

_____

_____

_____

_____

Second Round Tapping Topic: _____

_____

Rating Before Tapping (0-10): _____

Rating After Tapping (0-10): _____

What feelings or emotions came up for me? _____

_____

_____

_____

_____

_____

_____

_____

_____

_____

What other issues that came up for me while tapping?_____

_____

_____

_____

_____

_____

_____

_____

What do I want to tap about next time? _____

_____

_____

_____

_____

_____

Notes: _____

Date: _____

What issues, feelings, anxiety or stress am I experiencing right now?

_____

_____

_____

_____

_____

_____

_____

_____

Tapping Topic: _____

_____

Rating Before Tapping (0-10): _____

Rating After Tapping (0-10): _____

What feelings or emotions came up for me while tapping?

_____

_____

_____

_____

_____

_____

_____

Second Round Tapping Topic: _____

_____

Rating Before Tapping (0-10): _____

Rating After Tapping (0-10): _____

What feelings or emotions came up for me? _____

_____

_____

_____

_____

_____

_____

_____

_____

_____

What other issues that came up for me while tapping?_____

_____

_____

_____

_____

_____

_____

What do I want to tap about next time? _____

_____

_____

_____

_____

_____

Notes: _____

_____

_____

_____

_____

_____

_____

_____

_____

_____

_____

_____

_____

_____

Date: _____

What issues, feelings, anxiety or stress am I experiencing right now?

_____

_____

_____

_____

_____

_____

_____

_____

Tapping Topic: _____

_____

Rating Before Tapping (0-10): _____

Rating After Tapping (0-10): _____

What feelings or emotions came up for me while tapping?

_____

_____

_____

_____

_____

_____

_____

Second Round Tapping Topic: _____

_____

Rating Before Tapping (0-10): _____

Rating After Tapping (0-10): _____

What feelings or emotions came up for me? _____

_____

_____

_____

_____

_____

_____

_____

_____

_____

What other issues that came up for me while tapping?_____

_____

_____

_____

_____

_____

_____

_____

What do I want to tap about next time? _____

_____

_____

_____

_____

_____

Notes: _____

_____

_____

_____

_____

_____

_____

_____

_____

_____

_____

_____

_____

_____

Date: _____

What issues, feelings, anxiety or stress am I experiencing right now?

_____

_____

_____

_____

_____

_____

_____

_____

Tapping Topic: _____

_____

Rating Before Tapping (0-10): _____

Rating After Tapping (0-10): _____

What feelings or emotions came up for me while tapping?

_____

_____

_____

_____

_____

_____

_____

_____

Second Round Tapping Topic: _____

_____

Rating Before Tapping (0-10): _____

Rating After Tapping (0-10): _____

What feelings or emotions came up for me? _____

_____

_____

_____

_____

_____

_____

_____

_____

_____

What other issues that came up for me while tapping?_____

_____

_____

_____

_____

_____

_____

What do I want to tap about next time? _____

_____

_____

_____

_____

_____

Notes: _____

_____

_____

_____

_____

_____

_____

_____

_____

_____

_____

_____

_____

_____

Date: _____

What issues, feelings, anxiety or stress am I experiencing right now?

_____

_____

_____

_____

_____

_____

_____

Tapping Topic: _____

_____

Rating Before Tapping (0-10): _____

Rating After Tapping (0-10): _____

What feelings or emotions came up for me while tapping?

_____

_____

_____

_____

_____

_____

_____

Second Round Tapping Topic: _____

_____

Rating Before Tapping (0-10): _____

Rating After Tapping (0-10): _____

What feelings or emotions came up for me? _____

_____

_____

_____

_____

_____

_____

_____

_____

_____

_____

What other issues that came up for me while tapping?_____

_____

_____

_____

_____

_____

_____

_____

What do I want to tap about next time? _____

_____

_____

_____

_____

_____

Notes: _____

_____

_____

_____

_____

_____

_____

_____

_____

_____

_____

_____

_____

_____

Date: _____

What issues, feelings, anxiety or stress am I experiencing right now?

_____

_____

_____

_____

_____

_____

_____

_____

Tapping Topic: _____

_____

Rating Before Tapping (0-10): _____

Rating After Tapping (0-10): _____

What feelings or emotions came up for me while tapping?

_____

_____

_____

_____

_____

_____

_____

Second Round Tapping Topic: _____

_____

Rating Before Tapping (0-10): _____

Rating After Tapping (0-10): _____

What feelings or emotions came up for me? _____

_____

_____

_____

_____

_____

_____

_____

_____

_____

What other issues that came up for me while tapping?_____

_____

_____

_____

_____

_____

_____

_____

What do I want to tap about next time? _____

_____

_____

_____

_____

_____

Notes: _____

_____

_____

_____

_____

_____

_____

_____

_____

_____

_____

_____

_____

_____

Date: _____

What issues, feelings, anxiety or stress am I experiencing right now?

_____

_____

_____

_____

_____

_____

_____

_____

Tapping Topic: _____

_____

Rating Before Tapping (0-10): _____

Rating After Tapping (0-10): _____

What feelings or emotions came up for me while tapping?

_____

_____

_____

_____

_____

_____

_____

Second Round Tapping Topic: _____

_____

Rating Before Tapping (0-10): _____

Rating After Tapping (0-10): _____

What feelings or emotions came up for me? _____

_____

_____

_____

_____

_____

_____

_____

_____

_____

What other issues that came up for me while tapping?_____

_____

_____

_____

_____

_____

_____

_____

What do I want to tap about next time? _____

_____

_____

_____

_____

_____

Notes: _____

_____

_____

_____

_____

_____

_____

_____

_____

_____

_____

_____

_____

_____

Date: _____

What issues, feelings, anxiety or stress am I experiencing right now?

_____

_____

_____

_____

_____

_____

_____

_____

Tapping Topic: _____

_____

Rating Before Tapping (0-10): _____

Rating After Tapping (0-10): _____

What feelings or emotions came up for me while tapping?

_____

_____

_____

_____

_____

_____

_____

_____

Second Round Tapping Topic: _____

_____

Rating Before Tapping (0-10): _____

Rating After Tapping (0-10): _____

What feelings or emotions came up for me? _____

_____

_____

_____

_____

_____

_____

_____

_____

_____

What other issues that came up for me while tapping?_____

_____

_____

_____

_____

_____

_____

_____

What do I want to tap about next time? _____

_____

_____

_____

_____

_____

Notes: _____

Date: _____

What issues, feelings, anxiety or stress am I experiencing right now?

_____

_____

_____

_____

_____

_____

_____

Tapping Topic: _____

_____

Rating Before Tapping (0-10): _____

Rating After Tapping (0-10): _____

What feelings or emotions came up for me while tapping?

_____

_____

_____

_____

_____

_____

_____

Second Round Tapping Topic: _____

_____

Rating Before Tapping (0-10): _____

Rating After Tapping (0-10): _____

What feelings or emotions came up for me? _____

_____

_____

_____

_____

_____

_____

_____

_____

_____

What other issues that came up for me while tapping?_____

_____

_____

_____

_____

_____

_____

What do I want to tap about next time? _____

_____

_____

_____

_____

_____

Notes: _____

_____

_____

_____

_____

_____

_____

_____

_____

_____

_____

_____

_____

_____

Date: _____

What issues, feelings, anxiety or stress am I experiencing right now?

_____

_____

_____

_____

_____

_____

_____

Tapping Topic: _____

_____

Rating Before Tapping (0-10): _____

Rating After Tapping (0-10): _____

What feelings or emotions came up for me while tapping?

_____

_____

_____

_____

_____

_____

_____

Second Round Tapping Topic: _____

_____

Rating Before Tapping (0-10): _____

Rating After Tapping (0-10): _____

What feelings or emotions came up for me? _____

_____

_____

_____

_____

_____

_____

_____

_____

_____

What other issues that came up for me while tapping?_____

_____

_____

_____

_____

_____

_____

_____

What do I want to tap about next time? _____

_____

_____

_____

_____

_____

Notes: _____

_____

_____

_____

_____

_____

_____

_____

_____

_____

_____

_____

_____

_____

Date: _____

What issues, feelings, anxiety or stress am I experiencing right now?

_____

_____

_____

_____

_____

_____

_____

_____

Tapping Topic: _____

_____

Rating Before Tapping (0-10): _____

Rating After Tapping (0-10): _____

What feelings or emotions came up for me while tapping?

_____

_____

_____

_____

_____

_____

_____

_____

Second Round Tapping Topic: _____

_____

Rating Before Tapping (0-10): _____

Rating After Tapping (0-10): _____

What feelings or emotions came up for me? _____

_____

_____

_____

_____

_____

_____

_____

_____

_____

What other issues that came up for me while tapping?_____

_____

_____

_____

_____

_____

_____

_____

What do I want to tap about next time? _____

_____

_____

_____

_____

_____

Notes: _____

_____

_____

_____

_____

_____

_____

_____

_____

_____

_____

_____

_____

Printed in Great Britain
by Amazon